Daniel And The French Robot

The French café

It was a hot sunny afternoon and Daniel's friends came round for a drink.

The French robot led them into the garden and told them to pretend they were ordering a drink in a lovely outside French café.

The French robot pretended to be a waiter:

The French robot told them that there were the following drinks:

 **une limonade**

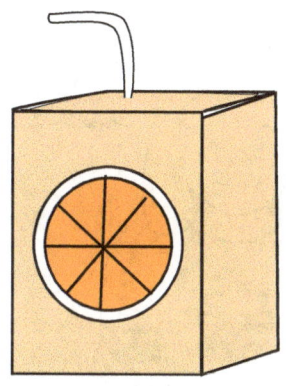 **un jus d'orange**

 **un jus de pomme**

Daniel had seen they also had coke, so he whispered to his friends that there was also:

 **un coca**

Emily ordered in French a lemonade:

Mathew ordered in French an orange juice:

And Daniel ordered in French a coke:

The French robot went away and came back with:

But had he got the drinks order right?

une limonade

Une limonade ..... now that was for Emily.

un jus d'orange

Un jus d'orange …. now that was for Matthew.

un jus de pomme

Emily had **une limonade**.

Matthew had **un jus d'orange**.

And Daniel had ordered **un coca** NOT **un jus de pomme**!

Once again Daniel asked for a coke:

Un coca, s'il vous plaît.

The French robot had hoped Daniel would forget he'd ordered a coke as it was healthier to drink fruit juice, but Daniel said again he wanted a coke. So the robot went away and got……

Un coca …. now **un coca** was for Daniel.

Daniel knew it wasn't as healthy as a fruit juice, but he hadn't had **un coca** for a while.

It had been such a fun afternoon!

Can you remember all the drinks we saw?
Let's say them together in French!

It was time to go home so they all said "**Au revoir**".

Daniel And The French Robot

Daniel's hobbies

After a few minutes, the French robot decided he liked playing mini-golf so he told Daniel:

J'aime le mini-golf.

The French robot knew Daniel liked football, but he wanted to hear him practise his French so he asked him:

Tu aimes le football?

J'aime le football.

Daniel knew how to say he liked football, so he replied in French "J'aime le football".

They then decided to play football. And the French robot told Daniel he liked football:

They ended up playing football together until they were both very tired!

They had done so much running around that the French robot decided to ask Daniel if he liked reading:

Now, there's something about reading that the robot really loved. All those fascinating stories and all those interesting facts, so he told Daniel:

They read together for a long time as they were having so much fun.

Daniel wanted to know why the robot didn't like swimming:

"Pourquoi?"

So the robot told him about the time he went swimming and he went rusty afterwards as he's made of metal!

The French robot liked skating. Daniel had got some boots with wheels on a while ago but he had found it hard. Maybe it was time to try them again!

The French robot held Daniel's hand and showed him how to skate. Daniel liked skating, so he told the French robot:

J'aime patiner.

After a while it began to rain, so they went inside.

The French robot asked Daniel if he liked singing:

"Tu aimes chanter?"

Daniel liked singing, so he replied:

"J'aime chanter!"

They switched on the radio, and sang lots of songs together. They sang together until Daniel was called for his dinner.

Daniel had told the French robot about the hobbies he liked. Let's say together in French what he'd said:

They liked a lot of the same things! It was a shame though that robots rust in water as Daniel liked swimming. Maybe he could get a special waterproof suit made for robots. What do you think? **Tu aimes nager?** (Do YOU like to swim?)

Useful French words and phrases

Useful French words

Bonjour! ---------------- Hello
Au revoir! --------------- Goodbye
Oui --------------------- Yes
Non -------------------- No
S'il vous plaît ----------- Please
Merci ------------------- Thank you

1	un (one)
2	deux (two)
3	trois (three)
4	quatre (four)
5	cinq (five)

Drinks

une limonade — a lemonade **un jus d'orange** — an orange juice **un jus de pomme** — an apple juice **un coca** — a coke

Hobbies

J'aime — I like   **Je n'aime pas** — I don't like   **le mini-golf** — mini-golf   **le football** — football

nager — swimming   **lire** — reading   **chanter** — singing   **patiner** — skating

Let's sing a song!

The following words could either be sung to a made up tune, or you could try saying the words as a rap. For inspiration of a melody to use you could hum first a nursery rhyme. How many different versions can you create using the lyrics?

une limonade, une limonade
s'il vous plaît, s'il vous plaît
une limonade, une limonade
s'il vous plaît, s'il vous plaît

un coca, un coca
s'il vous plaît, s'il vous plaît
un coca, un coca
s'il vous plaît, s'il vous plaît

un jus d'orange, un jus d'orange
s'il vous plaît, s'il vous plaît
un jus d'orange, un jus d'orange
s'il vous plaît, s'il vous plaît

un jus de pomme, un jus de pomme
s'il vous plaît, s'il vous plaît
un jus de pomme, un jus de pomme
s'il vous plaît, s'il vous plaît

Now pretend to order a drink in a lovely outside French café! One person will be the waiter / waitress and one person will be the customer. You can change une limonade to a different drink if you want to.

Waiter / Waitress: Bonjour
Customer: Une limonade, s'il vous plaît
Waiter / Waitress: Une limonade *(Pretend to hand over the drink the customer orders)*
Customer: Merci

© Joanne Leyland First edition 2017 Second edition 2018 Third edition 2021
The useful French words and phrases and the song may be photocopied by the purchasing institution or teacher for class or home use. The story may not be photocopied or reproduced digitally without the prior written agreement of the author.

www.ingramcontent.com/pod-product-compliance
Lightning Source LLC
Chambersburg PA
CBHW081359080526
44588CB00016B/2545